The Top Secret FILES OF MOTHER GOOSE!

BY **GABBY GOSLING** ART BY **TIM BANKS**

Gareth Stevens Publishing
A WORLD ALMANAC EDUCATION GROUP COMPANY

Please visit our web site at: www.garethstevens.com
For a free color catalog describing our list of high-quality books,
call 1-800-542-2595 (USA) or 1-800-387-3178 (Canada).

Library of Congress Cataloging-in-Publication Data

Gosling, Gabby.
    The top secret files of Mother Goose! / by Gabby Gosling; art by Tim Banks.
        p. cm.
    Summary: When "Mother" Goose tracks down the thief who stole the queen's tarts,
    she runs into several nursery rhyme characters.
        ISBN-13: 978-0-8368-3750-6 (lib. bdg.)
        ISBN-10: 0-8368-3750-9 (lib. bdg.)
        [1. Mother Goose—Fiction. 2. Mystery and detective stories.] I. Banks, Timothy, ill.
    II. Title.
    PZ7.G6765To   2003
    [E]—dc21   2003045714

This edition first published in 2004 by
Gareth Stevens Publishing
A Weekly Reader® Company
1 Reader's Digest Road
Pleasantville, NY 10570-7000 USA

This U.S. edition copyright © 2004 by Gareth Stevens, Inc. Text and illustrations
copyright © 2003 by Design Press Books, a division of the Savannah College of
Art and Design. First published in 2003 by Whitecap Books Ltd., 351 Lynn Avenue,
North Vancouver, British Columbia, Canada, V7J 2C4.

Design Press editors: Gwen Strauss, Carina Chocana, and Lisa Bahlinger
Whitecap editor: Kathy Evans
Gareth Stevens editor: Dorothy L. Gibbs

Cover and interior design by Design Press
Gareth Stevens art direction: Tammy West

Printed in the United States of America

2 3 4 5 6 7 8 9 10 09 08 07

This book is dedicated to
the Savannah College of Art
and Design illustration students,
whose work inspired this project.

ONE FINE MORNING, the Queen of Hearts went down to the kitchen to fetch her breakfast tarts.

"My tarts are gone!" she cried. "I smell a rat."

Of course, that was impossible. Pied Piper skipped town last year with the entire rat population and hasn't been heard from since.

The queen gathered everyone from the castle to question them about the missing goods.

The king said he knew nothing about the tarts. The jester said he knew nothing about the tarts. All the king's men said they knew nothing about the tarts.

"It must be that pesky knave, again," said the queen. "Off with his head!"

The Knave of Hearts, who had a reputation as a tart-lover, was suspiciously absent, and no one knew where he was. One of the king's men suggested that someone call Mother Goose to track down the culprit.

That's me — Mother Goose, Chief Detective of Nursery Rhyme Crime. I flew to the castle.

"So, Your Highness," I said to the queen, "I understand we have a situation with some tarts."

"A situation? I'll tell you the situation! My tarts are gone!" the queen said in a huff. She was a little cranky without her breakfast.

"And no knave, Your Majesty?" I asked the king.

"No knave," said the king.

"Any clues?" I asked.

"I'm clueless," said the king.

It didn't take a genius to spot the obvious — a trail of crumbs on the floor, an innocent-looking dish and spoon on the table, and a crumpled handkerchief.

"Hmmm," I thought to myself, picking up the hankie. It was embroidered with the letters HM. "Crumbs, a dish, a spoon, and someone's hankie. Looks as if I need to find this knave character and shake him down."

PRIVATE

CONFIDENTIAL

TOP SECRET

Wednesday, 08:00

Called to castle ("The Big House") by a sobbing Queen of Hearts. She claimed the Knave of Hearts stole a whole batch of strawberry tarts.

Does the knave have an alibi?

I reached the knave on his cell phone. Turned out he had a solid alibi. He was in Hawaii on vacation.

"You have any idea who the rotten apple might be?" I asked him.

"I wouldn't want to squeal," said the knave, "but, speaking of bad apples, Mary Contrary might have some information. Now, if you will excuse me, I have a hula lesson."

11

I thought about the knave's lead. Mary Contrary had a grudge against the queen. It all started with the strawberry festival, last year. The king and queen were judges at the bake-off. Mary tried to bribe the king with her strawberry tarts, but the queen caught Mary red-handed and gave herself first prize instead. Everybody knew the bake-off was fixed. The way I figure it, Mary had a score to settle.

"Ever seen this dish and spoon, Toots?" I asked Mary when I caught up with her.

"No, why?" she said innocently, tossing her head and jingling her bells.

I told her about the queen's missing tarts. Mary just laughed.

"Ever seen this handkerchief?" I asked her. "Looks like your initial on it — M?"

Mary shook her head. "I've never seen it," she said. "And I don't know anything about those tarts. Honest!"

I figured Mary couldn't have stolen the tarts without someone hearing her bells. Then I spotted what looked like tart crumbs leading to Mary's stand and beyond it.

"Thanks for your help, Doll," I said.

Mary Contrary

Runs a fruit and vegetable stand on the road into town. Rather grumpy. Wears silver bells and eats lots of strawberries.

Favorite food: homegrown vegetables

Criminal history: former member of the Pretty Maids gang

Following the trail of crumbs, I found Miss Muffet practicing yoga on her tuffet.

"Does that hurt?" I asked.

"It helps me relax," she said, "especially the pretzel posture. Would you like me to teach it to you?"

Miss Muffet was a little too eager. I declined.

"Ever buy strawberries from Mary Contrary's stand?" I asked.

"No, just blackberries," she said. "I can't eat strawberries. I'm allergic."

"I see," I said. "By the way, you didn't happen to lose this, did you?" I held up the handkerchief from the crime scene.

"Why, no!" she said, jumping off her tuffet. "Think of the germs on that thing!"

I thought she was going to fly the coop, but she was just running to the kitchen cabinet.

"I prefer paper tissues!" she said. "They're much more sanitary."

Miss Muffet pulled a can of disinfectant out of the cabinet and began spraying the air around the hankie. I know her type. She wouldn't eat tarts with just any dish or spoon. Then I saw the trail of crumbs leading away from the tuffet.

"I'll be on my way, Miss Muffet," I said, coughing through a cloud of disinfectant.

Little Miss Muffet

A yoga fanatic with a known fear of spiders. Also, a germ freak. And I'll bet my last dime that she doesn't eat sugar.

Favorite food: curd cheese and sprouts

Known allergies: strawberries and spider bites

The crumbs led me to Bo Diddle's place. Although it was late in the morning, Bo was barely awake. Keeps musicians' hours, I guess.

"Mr. Diddle," I began, but he interrupted me.

"Call me 'Bo,'" he said, rubbing his eyes. "Man, what time is it?"

"Sorry to wake you," I said, "but I'm here on business for the Big House. You know, Her Highness and His Majesty."

I pulled out the dish and spoon.

"Now, I know you recognize these two," I said. "What was in the dish, Bo?"

"Nothing, Detective Duck. . . er, I mean, Chief Goose," Bo stammered. "It was clean as a whistle!"

"I want the straight poop, Bo," I said.

"It's the truth, Ms. Goose! We were just having a little jam session at the castle. You know, making music. I used the dish and spoon to tap out a tune with Little Boy Blue. He was there before me. He might know what was in the dish!"

"Jam session?" I asked. "Strawberry jam, by any chance?"

Bo Diddle just gave me a blank look. My gut told me he wasn't our man, but he got me thinking about Little Boy Blue.

"He'll be asleep," Diddle informed me. "He sleeps all day."

I thanked him and flew off to Blue's place.

Bo Diddle

Plays fiddle with the legendary band, Diddle Diddle, whose last CD, "Over the Moon," went platinum in two days. According to one source, "Bo Diddle is one cool cat!" Seemed pretty much in the dark about the whole tart incident. Thinks Boy Blue might know something.

Habits: Often heard to remark, "Man, this place is jumpin'!"

17

Little Boy Blue

Fresh off the farm, but quickly shed his hayseed image and got a job blowing his horn with Bo Diddle's band.

Close friends: Bo Diddle and Little Bo Peep

Known allergies: hay fever

Habits: sleeps during the day and stays awake all night

Bo Diddle was right. Blue was still asleep when I got there — but not for long. He claimed he had never seen the hankie. Under questioning, he told me he had seen Little Bo Peep sneaking around outside the Big House the evening before.

"Maybe she knows something!" he said desperately.

"Maybe she did it, you mean?" I asked him.

Blue started to sweat. "I don't know," he said as he walked me to the door. "I'm no stool pigeon. That's your job."

I could see Blue didn't know a duck from a goose. Still, he had given me a hot lead.

Bo Peep was a little too easy to break.

"Miss Peep," I said, "I have an eyewitness that places you at the scene of the crime. What were you doing sneaking around the castle in the dark? Looking for a way into the kitchen?"

Peep's eyes sprang a leak, and she started sobbing.

"I was only looking for my sheep!" she cried.

I pulled out the handkerchief, but before I could ask her about it, she took it and blew her nose into it.

"That's tampering with evidence!" I squawked. But it was clear to me that Bo Peep was as innocent as a lamb. "Sorry to trouble you, Miss Peep," I said, "but I'm running out of leads."

Bo Peep looked up. "Well," she sniffled, "I know, there's, well, you might try the farmer's wife."

I told her the farmer's wife was missing. Peep hadn't heard the news.

"It's those three blind mice!" she said, and she looked like she might start crying again. "They were out to get her!"

"I know, Miss Peep," I said. "They're on the run and wanted for questioning. But that's another case."

"What about Patty Cake?" Peep asked, wiping her eyes. "He's a sworn enemy of the queen."

Peep had a point. If you were looking for someone who had it in for the queen, Cake would top the list.

"I like the way you think," I said.

I flapped my wings and hurried off.

Little Bo Peep

Cries easily and loses things a lot. Recent records show that she has enrolled her sheep in a pet obedience training class.

Favorite food: B-a-a B-Q

Favorite song: Baa. Baa. Black Sheep

21

Patrick Buttermore, also known as "Patty Cake," is the Irish baker. But why would a baker want to steal someone else's tarts? It just didn't add up.

"What do you know about the queen's missing tarts, Pat?" I asked.

Patty Cake smiled. "Why, nothing, Chief. Would you care for a sweet?" he asked, pointing to his pastries.

"Are you trying to bribe an officer of the law, Pat?" I asked sternly.

Cake's smile faded. "Of course not," he said.

"What do you have against the queen?" I asked, coming right to the point.

"Nothing!" Cake said defensively.

"Don't play coy with me, Cake," I said quickly. "Everyone knows you don't like her. I want to know why."

Patty Cake blushed. "Okay," he confessed, "I don't like that stingy queen. She always takes her sweet time paying her bill! But she's my best customer. I have to make so many strawberry tarts for her and Peter Peter that I can't stand the sight of the things."

"Peter Peter? I thought he ate pumpkins," I said.

"The wife eats the pumpkin," Patty Cake said. "Peter Peter can't resist a strawberry tart."

I couldn't arrest Patty for just disliking the queen. I figured my next stop was Peter Peter's place.

Patrick "Patty Cake" Buttermore

Irish pastry chef. Known throughout the kingdom for his elaborate, architectural cakes.

Dislikes the queen.

Hobbies: builds award-winning gingerbread houses

I found Peter Peter repairing a pumpkin shell.

"Patty Cake tells me you're a big fan of strawberry tarts," I said.

Peter Peter looked surprised. "Not me, not me!" he replied.

"Cut the double talk," I shot back. "I have proof that you buy strawberry tarts — lots of them."

"Well, yes, but not for myself, not for myself!" he stammered. "I don't like strawberry tarts. I buy them to give to the people who live in my pumpkins. I spend day and night, yes, day and night, passing out tarts."

"Anyone see you giving out tarts to your tenants?" I asked.

I figured he wouldn't lie about giving away free desserts on the night in question. I could easily check out his story.

"Sure, sure," he said. "Ask Humpty Dumpty. He got some. He hangs out with all the king's men, you know."

I thanked Peter Peter for his help.

Peter Peter "Pumpkin Eater"

His odd name comes from a habit of repeating himself. Grows giant pumpkins in his garden and hollows them out to make houses for poor people.

Habits: He has a very generous nature.

Close friend: Patty Cake He gives Patty Cake pumpkin meat for pies.

25

I tracked down Humpty Dumpty at his favorite waffle joint. Dumpty cracked easily under questioning.

"Yes!" he sobbed. "I know who stole the tarts!"

"Tell me," I demanded.

"No! You can't make me tell!" Dumpty blubbered.

Just then, one of the king's men approached. He had been sitting at the table behind us, and I had noticed him staring at the hankie. He looked worried.

"Excuse me, Ms. Goose, but what are you doing with one of the royal napkins?" he asked.

"What's it to you?" I sneered.

"Don't you know that's the king's linen?" he said worriedly. "You can get in big trouble for taking it from the castle."

Finally, everything started to make sense. My guess was that this crime was an inside job.

Humpty Dumpty

A hard-boiled character. Prone to accidents. Spends most of his time sitting alone. Can't seem to pull himself together.

Close friends: All the king's horses and all the king's men

Alias: Egghead

Known hangouts: diners and waffle houses

I realized that there was one person who knew all these characters — one person I had not yet questioned. I quickly returned to the castle to confront him.

"One of your men tells me this belongs to you," I said, holding out the napkin. "HM stands for 'His Majesty.'"

The king crumbled and confessed.

"It isn't fair!" he cried. "The queen has delicious strawberry tarts, while my pies are all full of four and twenty blackbirds. They taste terrible! I just couldn't take it anymore!"

The king told me the whole sad tale.

He had planned to eat just one tart, the night before, with the dish and spoon. But, unable to stop himself from eating more, he got scared. He sneaked out of the castle with the remaining tarts and ate them on the run, leaving a trail of crumbs behind him.

The king had to do some fancy explaining, and a punishment on top of it, to get back in the queen's good graces. Under the circumstances, I decided not to press charges.

The queen forgave His Majesty — eventually.